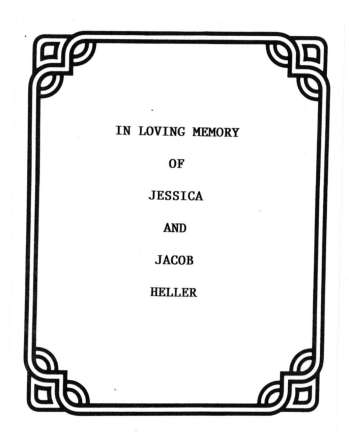

IN LOVING MEMORY

OF

JESSICA

AND

JACOB

HELLER

Baby Horses

Baby Horses

by Dorothy Hinshaw Patent
photographs by William Muñoz

 Carolrhoda Books, Inc. • Minne

Lovingly dedicated to Sandy
and all her babies that
give her so much joy

The photographer and author wish to thank
the many people who generously allowed their
horses to be photographed for this book.

This edition first published 1991 by Carolrhoda Books, Inc.

Library of Congress Cataloging-in-Publication Data

Patent, Dorothy Hinshaw.
    Baby horses / by Dorothy Hinshaw Patent ; photographs
  by William Muñoz.
        p.   cm.
    Summary : Describes the activities of foals in their first
  months of life.
    ISBN 0-87614-690-6
    1. Foals—Juvenile literature. 2. Horses—Parturition—Juvenile
  literature. [1. Horses. 2. Animals—Infancy.] I. Muñoz,
  William, ill. II. Title.
SF302.P37 1991
636.1′07—dc20   91-14662
                                                           CIP

Manufactured in the United States of America
1 2 3 4 5 6 7 8 9 00 99 98 97 96 95 94 93 92 91

17.50

Contents

Beginnings

Most horses are born in the springtime.

Some mother horses get help from people when they give birth. This baby is still partly covered by the sac that held him inside his mother's body.

The baby, called a foal, is wet.

The mother licks her new baby.
This helps fluff up and dry his fur.

The foal tries to stand up a few
minutes after being born.

Standing isn't as easy
as it looks.

12

The mother checks on her baby to make sure he is all right.

The foal tries again to stand. This
time he makes it.

A mother horse can help her foal
find his first meal.

Warm milk makes a strong baby.

Life with Mother

Running with Mother builds
strong legs.

19

20

It's fun to run with the other foals and
their mothers, too.

When Mother works, her foal
comes along.

Mother is good company.

It's nice to know Mother is there
when you are scared.

But sometimes it's hard
to get her attention.

Being Your Own Boss

Long legs make it hard to eat the sweet, tender grass.

Having long legs makes
it even harder to lick
salty ground.

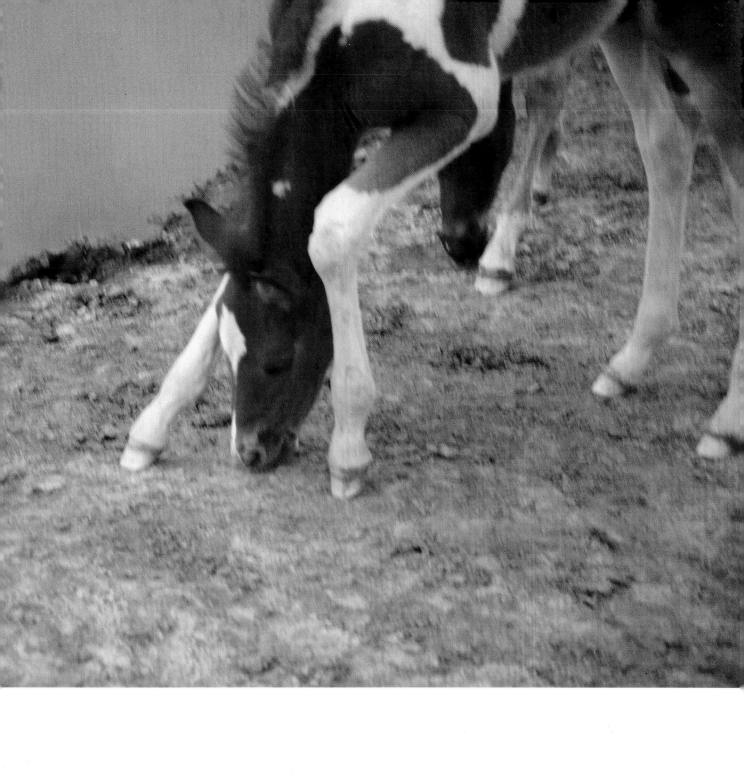

There's more than one way to scratch
an itch. Sometimes, a hoof will do the job.

30

Other times, teeth are the answer.

Trying to Be Grown Up

The spring air smells of grass
and flowers.

Getting everything to work right isn't easy when you're young.

34

Hay is hard to deal
with at first.

Is this bush good to eat?

How about this flower?

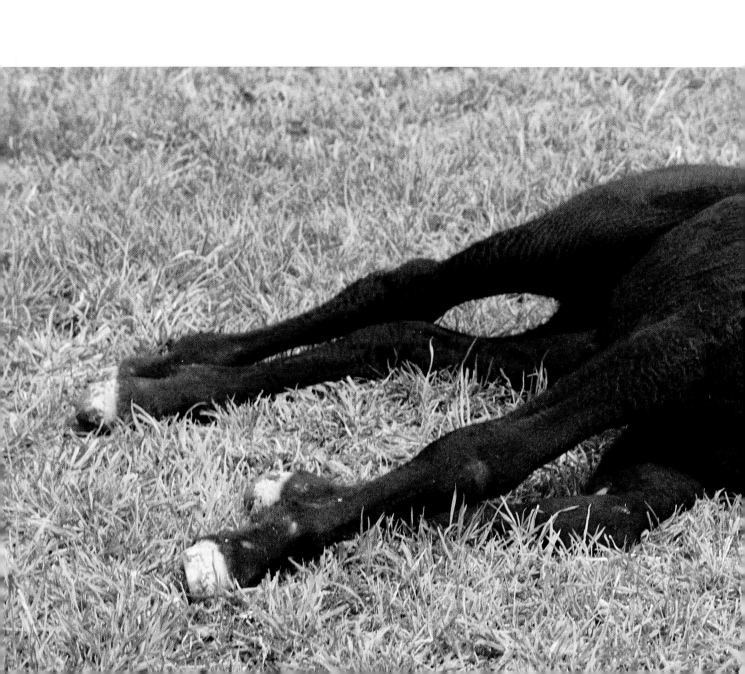

Exploring a new world can be tiring,
and babies need their naps.

Friends

As they grow older, foals spend more and more time away from their mothers.

42

Young horses have fun
exploring together.

They nuzzle each other
in greeting.

They nip playfully.

Foals like to run and play with each other.

47

Like grown-up horses,
foals enjoy grooming one
another, each nibbling
the other's fur.

Counting
on Yourself

Foals rear and kick in
the brisk morning air.

51

It's fun to run and jump, even when you're alone.

53

It doesn't take long to build strong muscles.

By wintertime, a mother's job is done.
Foals are on their own, with fuzzy coats
to protect them from the cold.

56